Draymond Green: The Inspiring Story of One of Basketball's Best All-Around Forwards

An Unauthorized Biography

By: Clayton Geoffreys

Table of Contents

Foreword

It's rare for an NBA legend to call a young rising star one of the top ten players in the league in just under three years of that player entering the NBA, but that is exactly what Jerry West did when he proclaimed that Draymond Green had broken into the upper echelon of basketball players during the 2015-2016 NBA season. Once just a second round pick, Draymond Green has quickly emerged as one of the next stars to play professional basketball. With an impressive ability to not only have a profound influence on the offensive end of the floor, but also on the defensive end of the floor, Draymond in many ways commands similar amounts of attention as his teammates, Stephen Curry and Klay Thompson. Already an NBA Champion, All-Star, and Defensive First Team member, the future is bright for young Draymond Green. Thank you for purchasing *Draymond Green: The Inspiring Story of One of Basketball's Best All-Around Forwards*. In this unauthorized biography, we will learn Draymond

Green's incredible life story and impact on the game of basketball. Hope you enjoy and if you do, please do not forget to leave a review!

Also, check out my website at claytongeoffreys.com to join my exclusive list where I let you know about my latest books. To thank you for your purchase, you can go to my site to download a free copy of *33 Life Lessons: Success Principles, Career Advice & Habits of Successful People*. In the book, you'll learn from some of the greatest thought leaders of different industries on what it takes to become successful and how to live a great life.

Cheers,

Clayton Geoffreys

Visit me at <u>www.claytongeoffreys.com</u>

Introduction

Not every star in the National Basketball Association comes out of a big-name college basketball program after playing a highly productive freshman year in what was essentially his tryout to be selected in the top 10 of the NBA Draft, thus earning a very lucrative, multi-million-dollar contract.

Sometimes, a basketball star is someone who wasn't even talked about as a potential NBA player when he was recruited to play at Michigan State University and played all four seasons in East Lansing, Michigan, not far from where he played high school basketball in his hometown of Saginaw. Draymond Green didn't draw an extremely large amount of national attention except for his big game performance in his NCAA Tournament appearances with the Spartans, which included a Final Four appearance. But he was selected in the second round by the Golden State Warriors, despite a lot of scouting reports stating he wasn't really expected to step up as a true contributor.

Those same experts probably didn't expect him to be one of a few players to record a triple-double in a series-clinching game to help Golden State win the NBA Finals in 2015 – joining greats such as Larry Bird and Magic Johnson. Green has made a name for himself through a lot of hard work and determination just to earn his time on the court with Golden State. But team scouts and the coaching staff saw and heard about that work ethic from his days at Michigan State and before that when he was growing up in a smaller town in Michigan, where his road to the NBA began.

Green's beginnings were much more humble than those of someone like LeBron James, who came straight out of high school and was instantly named the "King of the NBA." Green wasn't able to go straight from Saginaw to the NBA and even his early years at Michigan State were not yielding immediate success.

In fact, he had a lot of tough games where he looked weak. But through plenty of hard work and continuing the daily grind on the basketball court, Green evolved into a Big Ten Player of the Year as a senior.

He didn't get a lot of attention entering the draft like some of the other names from schools like Kentucky and Kansas, who by the way played only one or two years of college basketball. While he was drafted in the second round, his numbers were low as a reflection of his limited minutes. But he proved himself over time and has become one of the best starting centers currently in the league.

The proof is in his current contract, which is worth more than $80 million, and his NBA Championship ring; Green has had a lot of success in his young basketball career and there are a lot of reasons why he might build on that toward a Hall of Fame career. Time will tell, but there's a good chance if he maintains the pace he's had lately and continues to put in the same work ethic that he's maintained since his childhood in Michigan.

Chapter 1: Childhood, High School Years

Draymond Jamal Green was born on March 4, 1990, in Saginaw, Michigan, a town of about 50,000 people in the central part of the state. Green was raised by both of his parents, Mary Barbers and Wallace Davis. After a breakup between his father and mother, Green found a stepfather in Raymond Green. Draymond was part of a big family overall with three sisters – LaToya Barbers, Jordan Davis, and Gabby Davis – and two brothers, Torrian Harris and Braylon. Torrian also played basketball collegiately, at the University of Nebraska-Omaha for two seasons between 2009 and 2011.

There isn't a whole lot of information available about Green's family other than the fact that they all lived in Saginaw. It was a mid-major market at best with some semi-pro teams that were formed later on: the Saginaw Spirit in the Ontario Hockey League (started in 2002) and the Saginaw Sting of the American Indoor Football League (formed in 2008).

After spending his freshman year at Saginaw High School on the junior varsity team, he joined the varsity team, led by head coach Lou Dawkins, during his sophomore season, 2005-06. In his first season with the varsity team, Green averaged about 12 points and 11 rebounds a game. Green a member of a talented team that finished the season with an 18-4 record; that ended in the district playoffs with a 69-66 loss on March 8, 2006 to Arthur Hill – another high school team from Saginaw.

The team made a big improvement in the next season, finishing with a 25-1 record (undefeated in the Saginaw Valley League). Green averaged 25 points and 13 rebounds in his junior year for the 2006-07 season; he also had 3 assists and 3 steals per game. It was no secret that Green was one of the main reasons why the Saginaw Trojans advanced to the Class A

State Championship on March 24, 2007, with a 79-57 win over Redford High School of Detroit; Green was the star of the title game, scoring 27 points to go along with 8 rebounds and 7 assists. It was a great way to cap off a season in which Green converted on 52 percent of his attempts from the field while making 72 percent of his free throws. All of that earned him a spot on the Detroit Free Press and the Detroit News dream teams in 2007; Green also earned first-team spots on the all-area and all-league teams.

Before the start of his senior season, Green didn't want to waste any time deciding where his future was after high school. It wasn't an easy decision to choose which college he was going to enter after his days at Saginaw High School were complete. According to Yahoo's Rivals.com, Green had gained interest from 10 different programs, including basketball programs in the Big Ten Conference, the Atlantic Coast Conference, and the Southeastern Conference, along with some mid-major teams like Dayton and Xavier.

But on June 28, 2007, Green made his decision ahead of time by making his verbal commitment to join Tom Izzo at Michigan State University; Green officially signed his National Letter of Intent to play at Michigan State on November 14, 2007. He picked the Spartans over other finalist teams such as the Michigan Wolverines and the Kentucky Wildcats.

Green was just one member of a talented recruiting class for Michigan State, which was considered by Scout.com to be the 17th best in the nation as the Spartans were also able to get five-star recruit Delvon Roe out of Lakewood, Ohio, and four-star point guard Korie Lucious out of Milwaukee, Wisconsin.

So the question arose as to how well Green would play, considering he wouldn't be distracted by having to think about deciding where he was going to go to college and could help the Saginaw Trojans repeat as state champions. In his senior season, Green was averaging 20 points per game while also still keeping his rebounding average high with 13 per game and collecting 2 blocked shots in each contest – all of which are key reasons why he was named the captain of the Detroit Free Press All-State Dream Team while also being named to the Detroit News Dream Team.

On March 15, 2008, Green was the star again for Saginaw as he finished with 21 points and 19 rebounds in an impressive showing in his high school finale to help the Trojans win a second consecutive Michigan Class A State Championship with a 90-71 win over Pershing High School of Detroit. Afterward, Green's stock continued to grow in the various rankings for high school players. Green reached No. 36 on ESPN's 150 best high school seniors in the Class of 2008 while also finishing as the 13th ranked power forward in the country – all bonuses for helping lead a team to a record of 27-1 and earning a spot on the national high school basketball rankings (via *USA Today*) as the fourth best team.

Chapter 2: College Years

Freshman Year (2008-09 Season)

The Michigan State University Spartans have always been one of the best men's basketball teams in the country; thanks to the consistent winning ways developed by head coach Tom Izzo. Draymond Green was one of the new recruits for a team that was hoping to make a deep run in the upcoming NCAA National Championship Tournament after finishing 27-9 in the 2007-08 season, when they lost in the South Regional Semifinal to the top-seeded Memphis Wildcats.

It was a deep team and Green did not get a lot of minutes because Michigan State was led by star players like Kalin Lucas and Raymar Morgan. In the season-opening exhibition on November 5, 2008, at home against Northern Michigan, Green played just nine minutes near the end of a 118-57 blowout victory where he had 2 assists and 2 steals and made 1 of 2 free throws for what would have been his first official point of his collegiate career – although these games don't count toward his official totals because they were considered exhibitions, similar to preseason games. The same was true less than a week later, on November 10, 2008, when Green played 10 minutes to put up 2 points, 5 rebounds, and 1 blocked shot during the 112-69 exhibition victory over Lake Superior State.

Green scored his first collegiate field goal (2 points) near the end of the final six minutes of the Spartans' official season-opening win over Idaho, 100-62, on November 16, 2008; he also collected his first 2 rebounds while Chris Allen led the team with 21 points in just 19 minutes of action. Michigan State had a much more competitive game on the road at IPFW (Indiana University – Purdue University Fort Wayne) on November 19, 2008, in a 70-59 win on the road where Green was shut out in seven minutes playoff action.

Green spent a lot more time on the court as a reservist with 18 minutes during the first game of the Old Spice Classic in Lake Buena Vista, Florida, where Michigan State lost 80-62 to Maryland on November 27, 2008. He didn't score any points, missing all 3 field goal attempts, but he collected 6 total rebounds (5 on defense) to go along with 2 blocked shots. Maybe Izzo started seeing something in the 6-foot-7 power forward, as he got to play another 16 minutes in the team's 94-79 win over the Oklahoma State Cowboys on the second day of the Old Spice Classic on November 28, 2008; Green collected another 8 rebounds (5 defensive and 3 offensive) and 2 steals on defense while making 1 field goal and 2 of 3 free throws to finish with 4 points. However, Green played just 7 minutes, chalking up 2 points, 2 rebounds, an assist, and a steal during a 65-57 win over the Wichita State Shockers on November 30, 2008, on the final day of the Old Spice Classic. He followed that up by fouling out after playing only 6 minutes in the latter part of a 98-63 loss to the North Carolina Tar Heels on December 3, 2008, as part of the annual Atlantic Coast Conference and Big Ten Conference Challenge held inside Ford Field in Detroit, Michigan.

After the tough loss to the Tar Heels, Michigan State was able to finish off the rest of their non-conference schedule with a winning streak that started on December 7, 2008, when the Spartans defeated Bradley 75-59; Green scored 5 points (3 from the foul line) to go along with 5 rebounds, 2 assists and 1 steal. This was followed up with Green scoring in double digits for the first time with 10 points on a perfect 4 of 4 from the field and 2 of 2 free throws during the Spartans' 118-60 dominating victory over the Alcorn State Hornets on December 13, 2008; he also had 7 rebounds, 3 assists, 1 block and 1 steal. Green struggled to follow that up during the team's 79-65 win on December 17, 2008, over the Citadel (1 rebound and 1 block). In just 10 minutes during the team's big 67-63 road win over the Texas Longhorns on December 20, 2008, he had 4 points, 3 rebounds, 3 assists, 1 block and 1 steal. He wasn't needed much in the 82-66 win over Oakland Golden Bears on December 27, 2008, in the game right before the start of the Big Ten Conference season.

Green's minutes were limited on a very talented Spartans squad through most of the Big Ten Conference schedule with Michigan State dominating the competition for the most part – they lost just three games in all, against Northwestern (January 21, 2009), Penn State (February 1, 2009), and Purdue (February 17, 2009). But Green got some points here and there. During the regular season game on February 7, 2009, Green collected his first collegiate double-double during Michigan State's 75-47 victory over the Indiana Sooners; he made all 5 of his field goal attempts and 5 free throws to finish with 15 points while collecting 12 rebounds (9 defensive and 3 offensive) with a steal for good measure.

Outside of that, his presence wasn't truly felt until the Big Ten Conference Tournament in mid-March. The Spartans were the first overall seed in the tournament after going 15-3 during the regular season in the conference and ranking in the top 10 nationally. He played 17 minutes in the first-round game against the Minnesota Golden Gophers, a 64-56 win in which he made 2 out of 3 from the field to finish with 4 points, 5 total rebounds, 1 assist, and 1 steal. Green had a season-high 3 steals on defense against the Ohio State Buckeyes on March 14, 2009, at the Conseco Fieldhouse in Indianapolis, Indiana; he also had 4 rebounds and 2 points, while Kalin Lucas led the team with 17 points. But the Buckeyes would get the semifinal-round upset by a score of 82-70.

While Michigan State didn't get the automatic berth in the NCAA National Championship Tournament, the Spartans still received a higher seed among the 65 total entrants as an at-large team (hard to argue with a team that had a record of 26-6 at the time in one of the toughest conferences in the country). It was also a good fit for the Spartans to be placed as the second seed in the Midwest Regional bracket with their first few games held in Minneapolis, Minnesota.

During a first-round match with 15th-seeded Robert Morris University, Green scored in double figures by making 7 of 8 field goal attempts and 2 of 3 free throws for 16 points in 17 minutes while also collecting 3 rebounds, 1 assist, 1 steal and 1 blocked shot to help the Spartans get the 77-62 win on March 20, 2009. In the second round on March 22, 2009, during a 74-69 win over Southern California, Green made 5 of 8 free throws for most of his 7 points while leading the team with 9 rebounds (8 on defense) to help Michigan State advance to the Sweet 16.

Green scored another 7 points, making made 3 out his 6 field attempts in a very close and defensive battle while also collecting 2 steals to help Michigan State defeat the Kansas Jayhawks by a score of 67-62 at the

Conseco Fieldhouse in Indianapolis, Indiana, in the Midwest Regional semifinal. The Spartans then found themselves facing the first-seeded Louisville Cardinals in the Midwest Regional Final on March 29, 2009. Green played 24 minutes on the court while scoring 6 points, making 3 of 6 from the field and collecting 10 rebounds (8 while playing defense), 3 assists and 2 steals to help Michigan State get the 64-52 win as the Spartans advanced to the school's seventh Final Four appearance, along with the Connecticut Huskies (Big East Conference), the Villanova Wildcats (Big East Conference) and the North Carolina Tar Heels (Atlantic Coast Conference).

It was a return to Ford Field in Detroit, Michigan, for the Spartans and they would fare a little better than the loss to North Carolina earlier in the season. On April 4, 2009, during a semifinal to the National Championship, Michigan State got the 82-73 win over the UConn Huskies, when Green didn't have to play long to make contributions; he scored 8 points (3 of 4 from the field and 2 of 4 from the foul line) while also collecting 2 rebounds, 1 assist, and 1 steal in just 12 minutes. But the Spartans were unable to exact revenge over the Tar Heels from the ACC/Big Ten Challenge as Michigan State fell 89-72 in the National Championship on April 6, 2009; Green scored 7 points, making both of his field goal attempts and 3 of 5 free throws while grabbing 7 rebounds and 1 steal in 12 minutes on the court.

At the end of the season, Michigan State was 31-6 and had made it to the second spot on the Coaches' Top 25 Poll and eighth according to the Associated Press. Green averaged just 3.3 points and another 3.3 rebounds while making 55.6 percent from the field for the entire season. He finished with a total of 31 assists, 21 steals, and 9 blocks on the year in playing limited minutes for a talented Spartans team that would have every reason to believe they could make another run in 2010.

Sophomore Year (2009-10 Season)

Green started to see more minutes in some of the early non-conference games and his performances also improved. It started with a double-double in the season opener at home against the Atlantic Sun Conference's Florida Gulf Coast on November 13, 2009, as he scored 11 points, making 4 of 7 field goal attempts and all 3 free throws with 10 rebounds in Michigan State's 97-58 win. Green also had 3 assists in addition to 1 steal and 1 blocked shot against the Eagles in just 23 minutes of action on the court.

While the team was a decent mid-major program, the Spartans faced a tougher test early in the season on November 17, 2009, as they hosted the Gonzaga Bulldogs and got the hard-fought 75-71 win at home; Green made just 1 of 4 field goal attempts while making 4 of 6 free throws to finish with 6 points. However, he collected 10 rebounds for the second consecutive game.

The Spartans had an easier couple of game after that, starting with a 75-62 win over Mid-American Conference foe Toledo, in which Green played 30 minutes and made the most of it by sinking 6 of 10 field goal attempts and 3 of 6 free throws to finish with 15 points, along with 8 rebounds, 4 assists, 2 blocked shots, and 1 steal. A few days later, on November 22, 2009, Green was efficient in his offense with 4 of 5 field goal attempts converted for 8 points with 6 rebounds, 3 assists, 1 steal, and 1 block during a 90-60 blowout victory over the Valparaiso Crusaders.

Michigan State suffered its first loss of the season to another perennial tournament competitor from Florida on November 27, 2009; when the Gators got a 77-74 win. Green had one of his best games of the season with another double-double of 15 points and 11 rebounds to go along with 2 assists and 2 steals. Green also made 7 of his 10 field goal attempts for a decent night of shooting. The Spartans turned things around rather quickly on November 28, 2009, with a 100-68 win over the University of Massachusetts (also known as UMass) – a game in which he made 2 of 5 from the field to finish with 6 points, 7 rebounds and 6 assists. But they lost another close game to the pesky North Carolina Tar Heels on December 1, 2009, by a score of 89-82. Green made 4 of 8 from the field and 5 of 6 from the foul line to total 13 points with 7 rebounds, 2 assists, 2 steals, and 1 blocked shot.

Green finished the calendar year and the non-conference schedule with some big performances, starting with 12 points and 6 rebounds, making 6 of 8 from the field during the team's 72-60 win over Wofford on December 4, 2009. After another 9 points and 7 rebounds during a 69-52 win at the Citadel on December 7, 2009, Green nearly hit the 20-point benchmark on December 10, 2009, during an 88-57 win over the Oakland Golden Grizzlies when he made 9 of 11 from the field to score 19 total points, along with 12 rebounds. He reached this scoring mark again later in the month, when the Spartans had an 80-58 win over IPFW (Indiana-Purdue Fort Wayne) on December 19, 2009. In a 79-68 loss at Texas, he scored only 4 points. Despite the two tough games, Green scored 19 points by making 7 of 11 from the field and 5 of 7 field goal attempts during an 87-68 win over the Utah Utes on December 30, 2009 – he also collected 7 rebounds, 7 assists, and 3 steals.

The start of 2010 also marked the beginning of play in the Big Ten Conference, which was still considered one of the best in the country. The Spartans had a great start to their conference schedule on January 2, 2010, with a 91-70 win on the road against the Northwestern Wildcats in a game in which Green made all 5 attempts from the field and 3 of 5 free throws to finish with 13 points, 5 rebounds, 3 assists, and 4 blocked shots. This was quickly followed up with Green scoring 11 points by making 3 of 4 from the field and 5 of 8 from the foul line in a defensive battle on January 6, 2010, at home against the Wisconsin Badgers, a 54-47 win; he also collected 5 rebounds and

3 assists in the game. On January 9, 2010, Green had another double-double on the road in a 71-53 win over the Iowa Hawkeyes by scoring 14 points – 6 of 9 from the field, 2 of 2 from the foul line – while collecting 11 rebounds, 4 assists, and a steal.

The rest of January was a mixed bag of results: Green had only one more game scoring in double digits, finishing with 10 points on 5 of 6 shooting from the field during the team's 57-56 win over the rival Michigan Wolverines on January 26, 2010. He was close to two more double-doubles in the month of January; including 9 points and 11 rebounds during the Spartans' 70-63 win at home over the Iowa Hawkeyes on January 20, 2010, and again with another 9 points and 11 rebounds in a 79-70 win against Northwestern on January 30, 2010. Despite some games where he would score as low as 4 points (January 23, 2010, during 65-64 win at Minnesota), Michigan State started the Big Ten schedule with a perfect 9-0 record.

February was a month that head coach Tom Izzo was likely happy to get out of with a record of 3-4. The Spartans suffered their first conference loss on February 2, 2010, at Wisconsin by a score of 67-49; Green made 3 of 6 from the field for 6 points, 5 rebounds, 2 blocks, and 1 steal. It was the beginning of a three-game losing streak that continued on the road against the Illinois Fighting Illini in a 78-73 loss on February 6, 2010 – although Green had a really good game making 7 of 9 from the field and 3 of 4 from the foul line to finish with 17 points and 16 rebounds (10 on defense) along with 3 assists. While Green had a great game against Illinois, his performance went in the complete opposite direction on February 9, 2010, during a 76-64 loss to the Purdue Boilermakers, when he made just 1 field goal out of 13 attempts and totaled 6 points by making 4 of 6 free throws. Green had his worst performance of the season on February 13, 2010, when he missed all 7 field goal attempts and his 2 points came from the foul line against the Penn State

Nittany Lions; the Spartans still won 65-54 for a key road win.

But Michigan State won four of their last five regular-season conference games and Green had one of his best statistical runs starting on February 16, 2010, with a perfect 5 of 5 from the field with 4 of 6 free throws to finish with 14 points, 4 rebounds, 3 assists and 1 steal as the Spartans defeated the Indiana Hoosiers 72-58 – all in just 19 minutes of playing time. This was followed by 11 points and 5 rebounds in a 74-67 loss against the Ohio State Buckeyes. Green had another double-double with 12 points and 11 rebounds, shooting 50 percent from the field (six of 12 attempts) during a 53-44 win at Purdue. Green he then scored another 14 points, with 9 rebounds and 4 assists during a 67-65 win over the Penn State Nittany Lions on March 4, 2010. Green was given some rest with just 18 minutes of time during the Spartans' 64-48 win over Michigan on March 7, 2010; he only had 2 points, 3 rebounds, 1 steal, and 1 blocked shot.

Michigan State finished the Big Ten regular season with a 14-4 record and, while they were tied with the Ohio State Buckeyes and Purdue Boilermakers in terms of wins and losses, both of those schools had earned tiebreakers over the Spartans. The Buckeyes were given the regular-season title because of a 2-1 record over the Boilermakers and Spartans. Michigan State had the third seed overall and were able to get an opening-round bye in the Big Ten Conference Tournament. But they were upset in overtime, 72-67, by the Minnesota Golden Gophers on March 12, 2010; Green had a decent game himself, making 4 of 9 to finish with 10 points, 11 rebounds, 2 assists, 2 steals, and 1 blocked shot on defense. The early loss did hurt the Spartans' prospects of a berth in the NCAA National Championship Tournament – but not by much.

The Spartans still received an at-large bid and were placed in the Midwest Regional bracket; but the overtime loss to Minnesota dropped them down to a fifth seed in the tournament. Even though they were placed in the Midwest Region, Michigan State started the tournament at the Spokane Veterans Memorial Arena in Spokane, Washington, on March 19, 2010, with a 70-67 win over 12th-seeded New Mexico State; that was a game in which Green was extremely effective on the boards with 12 total rebounds (10 on defense) but struggled offensively with 2 points from free throws while missing his 3 attempts from the field. In the second round against the Maryland Terrapins (the 20th-ranked team in the nation), the Spartans got a key 85-83 win on March 21, 2010 where Green had 9 points, 8 rebounds, 5 assists, 2 blocks, and 1 steal.

As the tournament continued, the competition got a lot tougher for the Spartans as they faced a potential mid-major Cinderella in the ninth-seeded Northern Iowa Panthers during the Sweet Sixteen matchup on March 26, 2010, at the Edward Jones Dome in St. Louis, Missouri. It was a tough defensive battle; Green scored just 8 points, making only 1 field goal out of 8 attempts and 6 of 8 from the foul line. He still made some plays on the court with 5 rebounds, 4 assists, 2 blocked shots, and 1 steal as Michigan State held off Northern Iowa 59-52 to advance to the Elite Eight round. On March 28, 2010, the Spartans were taken to the limit by the Tennessee Volunteers in St. Louis during a 70-69 win for Michigan State to return to the Final Four once again. Green made 5 of 10 field goal attempts and all 3 of his free throws to finish with 13 points with 2 assists, 2 blocks, 1 steal, and just 1 rebound.

Michigan State went to Lucas Oil Stadium in Indianapolis, Indiana, for the national semifinals, along with the Duke Blue Devils, the West Virginia Mountaineers, and the Butler Bulldogs, who were entering their first Final Four in school history. The Spartans faced the Bulldogs on April 3, 2010, and it was a defensive war once again; Butler got the 52-50 win to advance to the National Championship, where they fell to Duke 61-59. During Michigan State's loss to Butler, Green played a total of 29 minutes and made 4 of 9 from the field and another 4 of 8 from the foul line to finish with 12 points to go along with 6 rebounds, 2 blocks, 1 steal, and 1 assist.

Michigan State finished the season with a record of 28-9 and their final ranking was fourth in the Coaches Poll and 13th in the Associated Press pool. Green's numbers saw a big increase from his freshman season with per-game averages of 9.9 points, 7.7 rebounds (third in the Big Ten), 3 assists, and about 1 steal and 1 block. While his field goal percentage went down to about 52.5 percent, his accuracy from the foul line improved from 61.5 percent as a freshman to 67.2 percent in his second year at Michigan State. That isn't bad for someone who only started three times while appearing in all 37 of the Spartans' games.

With those numbers coming off the bench for virtually the entire season, Green had the honor of being the first Michigan State player to be awarded the Big Ten Conference's Sixth Man of the Year Award by a wide margin. He was also given that same honor by Yahoo Sports. The local media named Green the Most Valuable Player for Michigan State. As for in-house awards, Green was named the Most Improved Player and the Chairman of the Boards (for rebounding) and was given the Antonio Smith Glue and Guts Award. Moving forward, those numbers would continue to grow as Green would become a much more integral part of the Spartans program.

Junior Year (2010-11 Season)

Because he had done so well in his sophomore year, Green became a co-captain of the Michigan State team. Unfortunately, this was not the Spartans' best season, as they finished with a 19-15 record; although it didn't feel like Michigan State would have that type of season in the early going.

After winning their exhibition games against non-Division I programs like Saginaw Valley State (88-44) and Nebraska-Omaha (102-72), the Spartans were ranked second in the nation entering their official season opener on November 12, 2010, at home against Mid-American Conference team Eastern Michigan. Green scored 12 points, making 4 of 6 from the field (including 1 of 2 from behind the 3-point line) and 3 of 5 free throws to help the Spartans get the 96-66 win. Green also collected 7 assists, 3 blocks, and 1 steal in just 24 minutes.

Less than a week later, on November 16, 2010, Green's numbers were bumped up to 31 minutes against the South Carolina Gamecocks at home; he made 5 of 6 field goal attempts (including 2 of 3 from 3-point range) and another 6 of 9 free throws to finish with 18 points and 12 rebounds for his first double-double of the season. Green also had 6 steals and 4 blocks to help the Spartans get the 82-73 win. Green continues to do well in the next game on November

22, 2010, against the Chaminade Silverswords of NCAA Division II as part of the annual Maui Invitational tournament. Green made 4 of 8 field goal attempts with just 1 of 4 free throws to finish with 10 points, 10 rebounds, 4 assists, and 3 steals as the Spartans would get the 82-74 win in the tournament's first round.

Unfortunately, Michigan State suffered their first loss in the second round of the Maui Invitational to the UConn Huskies, 70-67, on November 23, 2010. Green did have a big performance with 22 points, making 7 of 13 from the field, including 2 of 3 from 3-point distance, while converting 6 of 10 from the foul line; it was the first game in which Green scored 20 or more points in his collegiate career. In addition, Green collected another 15 rebounds, 5 assists, 3 blocks, and 1 steal. It was a tough loss, but it was against a Huskies program that would eventually climb the rankings and win the National Championship at the end of the season against the Butler Bulldogs, 53-41, on April 4, 2011. The Spartans were able to bounce back against then the 13th ranked Washington Huskies on November 24, 2010, during the third-place game of the invitational with a 76-71 win; Green had 12 points, 6 rebounds, 2 steals, 1 block, and 1 assist while making just 5 of 9 from the field.

After returning from Hawaii, the Spartans gained an easy win, 73-55, over Tennessee Tech on November 28, 2010. Green only played 23 minutes and made 4 of 8 from the field to finish with 10 points, 9 rebounds, 6 assists, and 2 steals. But it wasn't long until the Spartans suffered another loss to a quality opponent on the road against the Duke Blue Devils on December 1, 2010, as part of the annual ACC-Big Ten Challenge, 84-79. Green played well with 16 points on 6 of 11 from the field – with 3 of 5 beyond the 3-point arc – and also collected 6 rebounds, 3 steals, and 3 blocks against the team that was ranked on the top of the national polls at that point in the season.

Losses were coming against the ranked teams in the nation and the Spartans finally fell from being the second-ranked team to sixth, followed by a much needed 74-39 win over the Bowling Green Falcons on December 4, 2010, when Green had 10 points, 12 rebounds, and 5 assists. But it wasn't long before the Spartans suffered another loss to the eighth-ranked Syracuse Orange, 72-58, when Green had one of his worst games of the season, scoring just 6 points after making 1 of 6 from the field and 1 of 4 from the foul line – but he did have 11 rebounds, 5 assists, and 3 steals.

This was a common theme, with Michigan State defeating lower-ranked teams and having a tough time against the ranked teams in the national polls. After earning a 71-62 win over the Oakland Grizzlies (December 11, 2010) and a 90-51 win over the Prairie View A&M Panthers (November 18, 2010) – Green scored 11 points in both games – the Spartans fell to the 18th ranked Texas Longhorns at home on

December 22, 2010, by a score of 67-55. Green only scored 4 points and had just 8 rebounds and 1 assist.

After a very difficult non-conference schedule, the Spartans were able to bounce back with some strong wins at the beginning of the Big Ten Conference schedule; starting on December 31, 2010, with a 71-62 win over the Minnesota Golden Gophers, when Green made 6 of 11 field goal attempts to total 14 points, 6 rebounds, 4 assists, 4 steals, and 1 block. After a small New Year's break, the Spartans went on the road to defeat the Northwestern Wildcats 65-62 on January 3, 2011, in a game where Green converted on 7 of 11 field goal attempts while he had double-double of 15 points and 11 rebounds to go along with 4 assists, 2 blocks, and 1 steal.

But the Penn State Nittany Lions handed the Spartans their first conference loss on January 8, 2011, 66-62; Green made shot 20 percent from the field to score only 5 points to go along with his 10 rebounds, 6 assists, 3 blocks, and 2 steals. That was a tough loss that was almost repeated against the Wisconsin Badgers at home on January 11, 2011, where Green had his best individual scoring performance of his career with 26 points on 8 of 17 from the field, 3 of 5 from behind the 3-point line, and 7 of 9 free throws to help the Spartans defeat Wisconsin in a thrilling 64-61 overtime win; Green also collected 9 rebounds, 4 assists, 2 blocks, and 1 steal.

Michigan State then began a losing streak in the Big Ten that started with a 71-62 loss on the road against the Illinois Fighting Illini on January 18, 2011, when Green had 12 points, 6 rebounds, and 4 assists. On January 22, 2011, the Spartans fell to the Purdue Boilermakers, 86-76, in a game where Green was effective with 8 of 15 shooting from the field for 21 points, 11 rebounds, 6 assists, and 1 block. The streak continued at home to the big rival, the Michigan Wolverines, 61-57, on January 27, 2011; Green struggled with 9 points, 5 assists, 4 steals, and 3 rebounds during the loss.

The losing streak was snapped when the Spartans earned another thrilling overtime win against the Indiana Hoosiers, 84-83, on January 30, 2011, as Green had a dominant double-double with 19 points and 13 rebounds, sinking 7 of 15 field goal attempts (2 of 4 from 3-point range) and 3 of 4 free throws to go along with 5 assists, 2 steals, and 1 block. But Michigan State dropped their next two conference games with a 72-52 loss at Iowa on February 2, 2011, and an 82-56 loss at Wisconsin on February 6, 2011.

But Green became the first player in Michigan State basketball history to record a triple-double during the Spartans' 75-57 win on February 10, 2011; he made just 3 of 9 field goal attempts but sank all 9 free throws to score 15 points, along with 14 rebounds, 10 assists, 3 blocks and 2 steals. The victory streak was cut short by a 71-61 loss to the second-ranked Ohio State

Buckeyes on February 25, 2011, when Green had just 10 points, 6 rebounds, and 4 assists. Michigan State continued to struggle through the rest of the Big Ten Conference schedule, as they won just three of their last five games over Illinois, Minnesota, and Iowa before the beginning of the Big Ten Conference Tournament.

It was the first time in a long time that the Spartans had to play in the opening round of the conference tournament; they were usually getting that first day off while awaiting their first opponent. But Michigan State was hoping for a little late March magic to build stock toward an at-large bid for the Big Ten Conference Tournament at the Conseco Fieldhouse in Indianapolis, Indiana. On March 10, 2011, Michigan State got a 66-61 victory over the Iowa Hawkeyes with Green making 10 of 23 field goal attempts (1 of 4 from behind the 3-point arc) to score 21 points for another double-double with 14 total rebounds, 4 assists, 2 blocks, and 2 steals.

Their conference tournament success continued on March 11, 2011, with a 74-56 victory over the Purdue Boilermakers. Green only made 2 of 9 from the field and 3 of 4 free throws to finish with 8 points, but he collected 13 rebounds, 4 assists, 3 blocks, and 1 steal. But the tournament run was ended by their arch-nemesis Michigan on March 12, 2011, in a 70-63 defeat; Green played adequately with 10 points, 7 rebounds, 4 assists, 1 block and 1 steal.

The Spartans were 19-14 after their appearance in the Big Ten Conference Tournament and received a 10th seed in the NCAA National Championship Tournament – considering that the team's record was the result of how good the Big Ten Conference was in the 2010-11 season and how difficult the strength of schedule was, with games against Duke, Syracuse, Texas, and UConn. But the seeding placed them in the Southeast Regional bracket and a first-round game against the UCLA Bruins; who defeated Michigan

State 78-76 on March 17, 2011, at the St. Pete Times Forum in Tampa, Florida.

While Michigan State's season ended in the first round of the NCAA Tournament, Green did have a memorable performance in the game, making 6 of 13 from the field – including 3 of 8 from behind the 3-point line – and another 8 of 9 free throws to finish with 23 points, 11 rebounds, 10 assists, and 4 steals. Green became just the seventh player to record a triple-double during the National Championship tournament's history.

Of the 34 games that Michigan State played, Green started in 28 and averaged about 30.1 minutes of time on the court in his junior season. His averages improved to 12.6 points per game (second leading scorer), 8.6 rebounds (first on team), 4.1 assists (first on team), 1.2 steals, and just under 1 block per game. He led the team with 60 total steals on the season and set the school record for a frontcourt player with 141 assists. Speaking of being near the top of lists, Green was one of only 10 players in NCAA Division I to lead his team in rebounds and assists for the 2010-11 season. While his overall field goal percentage fell to 42.6 percent from the previous season's 52.5 percent, he went from 12.5 percent from behind the 3-point arc to 36.6 percent. He also boosted his free throw accuracy to 68.3 percent.

With all of those numbers, Green received some more individual awards for his junior season efforts. In the team awards, Green was given the Chairman of the Boards Award, named after "Jumping" Johnny Green, and the Stephen G. Scofes Inspirational Award. He also shared a portion of the Glue and Guts Award. Green was also named to the third team of the All-Big Ten Team that season.

Senior Year (2011-12 Season)

His senior year was Green's breakout season as a star for the Michigan State Spartans. He was a full-time starter in 36 of the team's 37 total games and he made quite an impact in the Big Ten. But it was a tough start to the season for the team after their two exhibition wins over Ferris State and Hillsdale.

On November 11, 2011, the Spartans faced the top-ranked North Carolina Tar Heels in a special season opener played on the *USS Carl Vinson*, an active supercarrier for the United States Navy that was parked at Naval Air Station North Island in San Diego, California, for the short-lived Carrier Classic that was planned as a special Veterans Day college basketball game. But the Spartans lost the game by a score of 67-55; Green stood out by leading all players with 18 total rebounds (11 defensive, 7 offensive) while shooting 6 of 19 from the field for 13 total points. The Spartans were then part of another neutral site game during the Champions Classic series that started that year, but Michigan State was unable to defeat the sixth ranked Duke Blue Devils in a 75-65 loss at Madison Square Garden in New York City, New York. Green struggled a little bit with 4 of 15 field goal attempts converted for just 10 points to go along with 7 rebounds, 4 defensive steals, 2 assists, and 1 block.

Those losses were against some of the best in the nation, but it would be a very long time before the Spartans took another mark in the loss column; they started a 15-game winning streak that extended through the rest of the non-conference schedule and into the early parts of their Big Ten Conference schedule. On November 18, 2011, Michigan State was able to get a decisive 76-41 win over Texas Southern, when Green made 5 of 11 from the field (2 of 3 from 3-point range) for 12 points, 11 rebounds, and 6 assists. A couple of days later, Green was a team leader in rebounds with 10 total boards – 9 on defense – to help Michigan State defeat Arkansas-Little Rock, 69-47, although he only converted 2 of 8 from the field, along with 5 of 6 from the foul line. After a few low-scoring games, Green scored 18 points by making 7 of 17 field goal attempts and 3 of 5 free throws to go along with 8 rebounds, 3 steals, 2 assists, and 1 block to help the Spartans defeat the Milwaukee Panthers, 68-55, on November 23, 2011. In their first official road game, the Spartans continued their dominance with a 72-40 win over Eastern Michigan on November 27, 2011; Green was efficient with 6 of 13 field goal attempts made to score 14 points with 13 rebounds for yet another double-double.

The success continued on November 30, 2011, during a 65-49 win over the Florida State Seminoles, as Green scored 16 points and 8 rebounds. But he became a team leader in different games in December. On December 4, 2011, Green led the team with 23 points after converting 10 of 18 from the field while collecting 10 rebounds, 4 assists, and 1 steal in a 110-68 win. After nearly getting another double-double with 14 points and 9 rebounds during the team's 89-69 win over Central Connecticut on December 7, 2011, Green had a career high of 34 points, making 11 out of 13 from the field, including 4 of 5 from the 3-point range, and another 8 of 9 free throws to help the Spartans defeat the Gonzaga Bulldogs on December 10, 2011, in Spokane, Washington.

Green had consecutive double-doubles in the Spartans' last three non-conference games that included 16 points, 10 rebounds, 6 blocked shots, 3 assists, and 1 steal to help Michigan State get the 90-81 win against the very talented mid-major program from Lehigh University – known for a recent upset in the NCAA Tournament – on December 22, 2011. Green's other double-doubles came in Michigan State's wins on December 17, 2011, against the Bowling Green Falcons (12 points, 10 rebounds) and on December 19, 2011, against Missouri-Kansas City Kangaroos (10 points, 11 rebounds).

The winning continued, as the Spartans handed the Indiana Hoosiers their first loss of the season on December 28, 2011, by a score of 80-65; Green had 11 points on 4 of 8 field goal attempts (made both attempts from behind the 3-point arc) while having 7 rebounds, 4 assists, 2 steals, and 2 blocks. A few days later, on December 31, 2011, Michigan State welcomed the Nebraska Cornhuskers to the Big Ten Conference by defeating them 68-55 in an impressive road win in which Green led the Spartans with 19 points by sinking 4 of 11 from the field (2 of 6 3-pointers) and converting on all 9 free throw attempts; he also collected 8 rebounds, 1 steal, and 1 block.

As the winning streak continued, it wasn't always easy because they were on the road against the Wisconsin Badgers on January 3, 2012, for a hard-fought 63-60 overtime win in which Green led the Spartans with 18 points and 14 rebounds, making 6 out of 19 from the field and 6 of 8 from the foul line. Green topped those performances on January 10, 2012, after a weeklong break in a home game against the Iowa Hawkeyes during a 95-61 win; he made 9 of 12 from the field (3 of 4 from 3-point range) to lead all players with 22 points, 10 rebounds, 5 assists, and 3 steals.

The streak was ended after 15 wins when the Spartans visited the Northwestern Wildcats on January 14, 2012, losing 81-74; Green had 14 points and 14 rebounds. However, the team was not able to bounce back in time for their rivalry matchup at Michigan, a 60-59 loss on January 17, 2012; Green struggled with just 3 of 8 field goal attempts made for 7 points while leading the team with 11 rebounds. He had an opportunity for a buzzer beater but missed a jump shot with one second left to give the Wolverines the upset win.

The Spartans wanted to forget those heartbreaking losses and reestablish themselves as the best team in the Big Ten. It started on January 21, 2012, when they hosted the Purdue Boilermakers for an 83-58 win, where Green once again led the team with 12 rebounds (all on defense) while scoring 8 points with 7 assists, 2 steals, and 1 block – the negative was that he didn't have a lot of scoring opportunities and went just 3 for 6 from the field. A few days later, on January 25,

2012, the Spartans jumped into a tie for first place in the regular-season standings with the Ohio State Buckeyes with a 68-52 win at home over Minnesota; a game in which Green was much better with 9 of 11 field goal attempts and a total of 22 points to go with 14 rebounds (12 on defense) and 6 assists. The momentum was short-lived, as they went on the road to Illinois for a 42-41 loss in which the only Michigan State player to score in double digits was Branden Dawson with 12 points and 13 rebounds; Green had only 5 points on 1 of 6 shooting from the field with 8 rebounds and 5 turnovers.

If Michigan State was going to make a run at a regular-season conference championship, they were going to have to go on another winning streak similar to the one after they lost to North Carolina and Duke at the beginning of the season. They were able to defeat their in-state rival Michigan in a revenge victory on February 5, 2012, by a score of 64-54. Green had yet another double-double, making 7 of 11 from the field for 14 points with 16 rebounds (14 on defense) with 4 assists and 1 steal in 38 minutes of action. A few days later, the Spartans defeated the struggling Penn State Nittany Lions 77-57 as Green had an impressive 23 points by making 6 of 15 from the field and 9 of 14 free throws; he also had 12 rebounds and 5 assists in the win. Green nearly had a third consecutive double-double during the team's 58-48 win over the Buckeyes with 12 points and 9 rebounds. But he had 20 points and 10 rebounds to lead the Spartans' in a 69-55 win over the Wisconsin Badgers on February 16, 2012. Keith Appling also contributed 20 points in that win.

Michigan State was on another roll as they then defeated Purdue in West Lafayette, Indiana, on February 19, 2012, in a 76-62 win; Green led the team in scoring with 20 points by making 7 of 15 field goal attempts (3 of 4 from 3-point range), followed by 17 points from Austin Thornton, 15 points from Dawson, and another 12 points from Derrick Nix from the bench. Green also had 10 rebounds and 7 assists at

Purdue. He was starting to become the power forward to lead Michigan State on a late-season run as he had 17 points to lead all players in the team's 66-61 win at Minnesota on February 22, 2012. Three days later, the Spartans defeated Nebraska 62-34; Michigan State had 9 steals as a team; led by Green with 3 to go along with another 20-point game as he sank 7 of 11 from the field, including 3 of 6 from behind the 3-point arc. Green also collected another 10 rebounds on defense to have yet another double-double.

The seven-game winning streak ended in Indiana with a 70-55 loss to the Hoosiers on February 28, 2012, despite Green scoring 29 points by making 10 of 17 field goal attempts (with 3 of 6 from 3-point range) and 6 of 7 from the foul line. No other Spartan had more than 8 points (Thornton) while the Hoosiers had five players score in double digits. Michigan State did have a chance to win the Big Ten regular-season title at their home court in the Breslin Center, but they were unable to hold off Ohio State on March 4, 2012, in a

72-70 loss as William Buford's go-ahead jumper with one second left was the deciding field goal. Green had another double-double after shooting 6 of 18 from the field for 19 points, 12 rebounds, 3 assists, and 1 steal against Ohio State.

The regular-season title went to a series of tiebreakers that featured the Spartans, Wolverines, and Buckeyes having a 2-2 record against each other. So the second tiebreaker was against the next highest-ranked common opponent in Wisconsin – which eliminated the Buckeyes. With the same record against the Indiana Hoosiers, the fourth and final tiebreaker went to how both teams did against the Purdue Boilermakers – Michigan State was 2-0 while Michigan was 1-1. So the Spartans did have the regular-season title and the first overall seed in the Big Ten Conference Tournament that was to be held at the newly named Bankers Life Fieldhouse in Indianapolis, Indiana.

After the first round-games were played, Michigan State faced the Iowa Hawkeyes in the quarterfinals on March 9, 2012, and earned a dominant 92-75 win; Green made 8 of 13 field goal attempts and 5 of 7 from the foul line to finish with 21 points, 10 rebounds, 5 assists, and 3 blocks. The next day, during the tournament's semifinals, the Spartans took care of the Wisconsin Badgers with a 65-52 win in a game where Green led the team in scoring with 14 points and in rebounds with 16– he also had 5 assists, 3 blocks, and 1 steal. Not only did the performance help Michigan State get to the Big Ten Championship game, he also passed Johnny Green for second in school history with 1,046 career rebounds (that number would obviously grow before his time as a Spartan would be over).

It set up a championship game between the top two-ranked teams in the conference, Michigan State and Ohio State. But the Buckeyes were not able to top the green and white this time as Green hit a key 3-point jumper with about 1:35 left in the game to help give the Spartans enough distance to hold off Ohio State in a 68-64 win on March 11, 2012; Green finished with 12 rebounds and 9 rebounds. Michigan State won the Big Ten Tournament title and Green was awarded the tournament's Most Valuable Player award after averaging 15.7 points, 11.7 rebounds, and 4.3 assists in the three tournament games.

Michigan State gained an automatic berth in the NCAA National Championship Tournament and was given the top seed in the West Region of the overall bracket (and considered the fourth overall ranked team entering the tournament behind the Kentucky Wildcats, Syracuse Orange, and North Carolina Tar Heels). In the opening-round game on March 16, 2012, against the Long Island Blackbirds, Green made more history with 24 points, 12 rebounds, and 10 assists for a triple-double that helped give the Spartans an 89-67 win over the 16th-seeded Blackbirds of the Northeast Conference. The performance put Green in pretty good company as only the third player in NCAA

Tournament history to record a triple-double – joining Oscar Robinson and Magic Johnson.

Green followed that up in the tournament's second round with 16 points, 13 rebounds, 6 assists, and 2 steals to help the Spartans defeat the ninth-seeded Saint Louis Billikens 65-61 on March 18, 2012, to advance to the tournament's Sweet Sixteen. It was then that the Spartans faced the fourth-seeded Louisville Cardinals, who were having an amazing season of their own, on March 22, 2012, at the U.S. Airways Center in Phoenix, Arizona. Despite Green having another double-double with 13 points and 16 rebounds, he only made 5 of 16 from the field (1 of 7 from 3-point range) that showed the Spartans' struggles with a 28.6 percent field goal rating for the 57-44 loss that ended their season with a record of 29-8.

At the end of the year, Green received a lot of national attention after averaging 16.2 points, 10.6 rebounds (ninth in the nation), and 3.8 assists for his senior season with Michigan State. He was named the Division I Player of the Year by the National Association of Basketball Coaches (NABC) and was named a consensus first-team All-American player by the NABC, the Associated Press, *Sporting News*, and other publications. He finished third in the voting for the John R. Wooden Award for best men's college basketball player while also being named to Dick Vitale's All-Solid Gold Super Seven team.

Green had a great four-year collegiate career and was one of only three players in Spartans' basketball history to finish with more than 1,000 points and 1,000 rebounds. Considering how good a program Michigan State has been, it's no surprise that Green was attracting some attention in the 2012 NBA Draft and declared that he would attempt to play basketball at the professional level.

Chapter 3: NBA Career

2012 NBA Draft

Most players who declare for the NBA Draft out of college are the type of players who spent their freshman year on campus only because of the 2005 rule change that said prospective players could not make the transition to professional basketball from high school. But Draymond Green was able to develop a lot during his four years at Michigan State, which has been known to produce a number of quality athletes under head coach Tom Izzo.

The NBA scouts were raving about Green's ability to make himself the glue of the team in addition to his strong rebounding skills that continued to grow as he got more time playing in East Lansing, Michigan. That's because he had a very large wingspan that fit the strong, 6-foot-7-inch and 236-pound frame. With his size and rebounding range, he also showed a lot of ability as an offensive threat, as his ability to set his feet and his rhythm made him a prototypical shooting forward. Scouts found that his ability to pass and get the ball out from the post to his teammates really developed in his senior year at Michigan State, which made it hard for defenders at the college level who were off the ball to try and keep their eyes on their assigned man and the ball simultaneously.

There were some concerns that Green might be great at the college level but never really excelled in any individual facets of his game. Some scouting reports stated that Green was undersized for his forward position while also having not as much athleticism as some of the NBA players in a similar role for their respective teams. Part of that is because some scouts claimed that Green didn't have the type of speed, agility, and elusiveness under the rim and wasn't really expected to be able to shake defenders off a dribble and had only a small amount of expected upside in the NBA.

There were a number of quality players who were also in the same 2012 NBA Draft class, with Anthony Davis of Kentucky being the consensus number one draft pick, who was selected by the New Orleans Hornets. He was followed by Michael Kidd-Gilchrist of Kentucky going second overall to the Charlotte Bobcats and Bradley Beal of Florida being picked up by the Washington Wizards. Green had a long wait as all of the teams in the NBA passed him by in the first round, with a number of Big Ten players being picked ahead of him, like Meyers Leonard of Illinois going 11th to the Portland Trail Blazers and Jared Sullinger of Ohio State at 21st overall by the Boston Celtics. Green was the third player out of the Big Ten Conference selected in the 2012 NBA Draft, but it wasn't until the second round when he was picked by the Golden State Warriors with the 35th selection overall – some calling Green a good valuable pick in the second round for someone who has the abilities to do a little bit of everything.

It was a decent draft for the Warriors, who had also selected Harrison Barnes, a 6-foot-8 small forward out of North Carolina, with the seventh overall pick and Festus Ezeli, a 6-foot-11 center from Vanderbilt, with the 30th pick to conclude the first round of the draft. Add the 7-foot-1 center Ognjen Kuzmic from Spain with the 52nd selection later in the second round and Golden State had a lot of expectations to make some improvements from the 23-43 record accumulated in the 2011-12 season. A number of NBA experts felt that, after the 2012 draft, the Warriors were starting to round out their starting lineup that needed stability after years of missing the playoffs while also adding some depth when the team had issues with injuries of their star players in Stephen Curry and Andrew Bogut in that 2011-12 season.

2012-13 Season

Green was a rookie who was going to get minutes coming off the bench on a Warriors team that had a starting lineup with Stephen Curry and Klay Thompson as the leading scoring threats and David Lee, Andrew Bogut, and rookie Harrison Barnes rounding out the starting five. In the first game of the season on October 31, 2012, Green played only a little more than one minute and had just 1 defensive rebound during the Warriors' 87-85 win over the Phoenix Suns. He struggled to score any points right away and got his first official point in the NBA on a free throw during Golden State's 101-77 loss to the Los Angeles Lakers on November 9, 2012. It wasn't until Golden State played at home against the Atlanta Hawks on November 14, 2012, that Green got his first field goal– he went 2 for 3 from the field to finish with 5 points in the 92-88 win.

The month of December was a good month for Green in terms of collecting rebounds off the bench. On December 7, 2012, Green pulled down 10 rebounds in nearly 28 minutes during a 109-102 win over the Brooklyn Nets; he was the only Warrior with double-digit boards behind the starter Lee's 15 rebounds; Green also had 3 steals and 3 assists in the game. One day later, while visiting the Washington Wizards, Green had another 8 rebounds to go with 6 points in a 101-97 win over the Wizards.

Green nearly got another double-digit rebound game on December 10, 2012, on the road against Charlotte with 9 total rebounds (7 on defense) to support Lee's 11 rebounds in the Warriors 104-96 victory over the Hornets. Green missed all 8 of his field goal attempts. Less than a week later, on December 15, 2012, Green had another 8 rebounds with 5 points on 25 percent shooting from the field in Golden State's 115-93 win on the road against the Atlanta Hawks. The only other game in which he was close to getting double-digit rebounds was when he collected 9 on February 9, 2013, during a 116-91 loss on the road to the Dallas Mavericks; a game where he scored 8 points by making just 3 of 8 from the field and both free throw attempts.

While Green was mostly known for being able to get rebounds coming off the bench, he did score in double figures for the first time on December 21, 2012, at home against the Charlotte Bobcats, when he scored 11 points by making 5 of 6 field goal attempts – 1 of 2 beyond the 3-point line – during the Warriors' 115-100 victory; he also 4 assists, 2 rebounds, and 1 block in the contest. Through the rest of his rookie season, Green had five games where he scored 9 points; including November 18, 2012, when the Warriors lost 119-109 and he made 4 of 6 of his attempts from the field (1 of 2 from 3-point range) to go along with 5 rebounds. On the very next night in Dallas, Texas, Green made 2 of 4 from the field and all 4 shots from the foul line for 9 points, 7 rebounds, 3 steals, and 1 assist during a 105-101 win over the Mavericks.

On February 27, 2013, Green made his first NBA career start in a game at Madison Square Garden against the New York Knicks. In a little more than 27 minutes of action, Green made 2 out of his 4 field goal attempts to finish with 4 points and also collected 5 rebounds, 1 assist, 1 steal, and 1 block. His teammate Curry was the one with the historic game, making 18 of 28 field goal attempts (11 of 13 from 3-point range) for 54 points, but the Warriors lost 109-105.

Green made appearances in 79 of the Warriors' 82 games and Golden State was able to advance to the playoffs after finishing 47-35 to finished second in the Pacific Division, which was good for the sixth seed in the Western Conference. During the regular season, Green finished with averages of about 13.4 minutes, just under 3 points and about 3.3 rebounds per game during his limited action. Now Green would make a few key contributions during the Warriors' 2013 playoff push.

After scoring just 2 points in less than five minutes in the Game 1 loss against the Denver Nuggets as part of the opening-round playoff series, Green's minutes improved over the next three games, which were all wins for Golden State. Green scored 5 points in the 131-117 win on April 23, 2013, in Denver, Colorado, and in a 110-108 win on April 26, 2013. But Green was a key player in the team's Game 4 victory on April 28, 2013, when he made 5 of 8 from the field, including 2 of 4 from 3-point range, to have 13 points, 6 rebounds, 4 steals, 2 assists, and 1 block to help Golden State get the 115-101 win and a 3-1 series lead. The Nuggets won Game 5 on April 30, 2013, with a 107-100 decision; Green had just 3 points in his 14 minutes on the court. The Warriors closed out the series on May 2, 2013, in a Game 6 win, 92-88, where Curry had 22 points to lead Golden State; Green was second in the team's scoring with 16 points, making 6 of 12 from the field (2 of 4 from 3-point range) and pulling down 10 rebounds.

Green maintained his scoring momentum in the first game of the Western Conference semifinals, making 3 of 8 from the field (2 of 4 from 3-point range) for 10 points to go with his 7 rebounds, 2 blocks and 2 assists during Golden State's 129-127 double overtime loss on May 6, 2013. Green started Game 2 on May 8, 2013, when he made 2 of 8 from the field for 5 points to go with 7 rebounds and 5 assists as the Warriors got the 100-91 win in San Antonio. After losing 102-92 to the Spurs in Game 3, the Warriors won 97-87 win in Game 4 on May 12, 2013, when Green only had to contribute 3 points while his fellow rookie Barnes had 26 points and Curry scored 22. But the Spurs took Games 5 and 6 to clinch the series and continue on toward the NBA Finals, where they lost to the Miami Heat in seven games. And, while it was a tough ending for the Warriors and Green couldn't maintain the offensive momentum he had built up with the 16 points against the Nuggets, his future looked brighter than it did during the regular season.

2013-14 Season

There were some major improvements made by Green during the offseason in an effort to have an even bigger impact in his sophomore season with Golden State. One of the first things coaches noticed was that he had dropped about 20 pounds. In addition, he had also improved his accuracy from long range and had become a better defender.

With the work he put in during the offseason, he earned himself some more time on the court. When he did shoot, he was making a higher percentage of his field goal attempts. During the season opener, when the Warriors defeated the Los Angeles Lakers 125-94 on October 30, 2013, Green came off the bench to make 3 of 4 field goal attempts, including his lone 3-point attempt for 7 points and 7 rebounds. Through most of November, Green scored points here and there, with a number of games where his limited attempts still yielded conversions of 50 percent or more from the field.

One of his best games early in the season came on November 22, 2013, when he made 4 of 5 field goal attempts (including 2 of 3 from behind the 3-point arc) to finish with 12 points while also collecting 4 rebounds and 2 steals; a great game coming in as a reserve, despite the Warriors losing 102-95 to the Lakers. But in the games that followed, he had stat lines that featured games with 7 or less points through the rest of the month of November.

While Green wasn't getting on the court as the main scoring threat, he was making big plays during his minutes off of the bench. During a road game against the Sacramento Kings on December 1, 2013, Green tipped in one of Curry's missed field goal attempts with less than 30 seconds left in the game as part of a comeback from 16 points down; Golden State held on for a 115-113 win. The tip-in accounted for 2 of Green's 9 points in a game in which he was 2 for 2 from behind the 3-point line and also had 5 rebounds, 4 assists, and 1 steal. Defense and rebounds were a big part of that month for Green, as he was showing his skills in collecting rebounds and blocking shots. For example, Green blocked 3 shot attempts during an 89-81 win over the Denver Nuggets on the road on December 23, 2013.

The month of December was tough, with a number of offensive struggles, including those on Christmas Day, December 25, 2013, at home against the Los Angeles Clippers. After missing all 3 field goal attempts and pulling down only 1 rebound in about 7½ minutes, Green was ejected from the game after committing a flagrant foul (level 2) on Clippers' star Blake Griffin. While the Warriors got the 105-103 win over the Clippers, Green got some bad news after the game when he learned that the league was fining him about $15,000 for not leaving the court in a timely manner after being ejected from the game by the referees. It didn't bother Green in the Warriors' next game on December 27, 2013, when he had 11 points, making 4 of 7 from the field (1 of 3 from 3-point range) and sinking both of his free throws to help Golden State defeat the Phoenix Suns, 115-86; Green also collected 6 rebounds in the game.

It was a while before Green scored in double digits; not until the team's 123-116 loss at home to the Nuggets on January 15, 2014. Green went 3 of 5 from the field and made both 3-point shots to finish with 11 points, along with 4 rebounds, 3 assists, and 1 steal. Green quickly followed that up on January 17, 2014, with another 10 points, 5 rebounds, 3 assists, and 1 steal during a 127-121 loss to the Oklahoma City Thunder. He continued to maintain his spot as one of the top reserve players on Golden State's bench, but that changed when David Lee suffered a hamstring injury that led head coach Mark Jackson to bring Green up to the starting lineup.

Now a starter, Green got his first double-double of the season in a 123-80 win over the Philadelphia 76ers on February 10, 2014; he had 11 points and 11 rebounds – 10 of which were collected on defense – while he blocked 4 shots. In the next few games, he had some near double-doubles, including 12 points and 8 rebounds during a 101-92 win on the road over the Sacramento Kings on February 19, 2014. Later in the month, Green had another double-double on February 22, 2014, making 5 of 16 from the field and 8 of 10 free throws to finish with 18 points, 10 rebounds, 3 steals, and 2 assists to help the Warriors get the 93-86 win over the Brooklyn Nets.

As the season entered the month of March, Green's productivity continued to grow. He averaged about 8 points per game while making 43.6 percent of his field goal attempts during that month. His best game of the month came on March 14, 2014, when he made 7 of 12 field goal attempts (2 of 5 from 3-point range) to score 18 points with 9 rebounds in a 103-94 loss at home to the Cleveland Cavaliers. It was a game that followed a 10-point performance during a 111-98 loss visiting the Los Angeles Clippers on March 12, 2014. His third double-double came on April 4, 2014, during a 102-69 win over Sacramento, when Green got the start and finished with 10 points, 10 rebounds, and 4 assists despite making just 36.4 percent of his field goal attempts.

Just as the regular season was coming to a close, Green had the best game of his career during Golden State's 130-120 win while hosting the Minnesota Timberwolves on April 14, 2014; he was one of four Warriors to score 20 or more points after he finished with 20 points (a career high), 12 rebounds (tied a career high), 5 assists, 4 steals, and 2 blocks while making 77.8 percent from the field (4 of 5 from behind the 3-point arc). Golden State finished with a lot of momentum and a record of 51-31. But the Warriors were behind the Clippers in the Pacific Division, who went 57-27. While the Clippers were the third seed in the Western Conference, they had to face the Warriors in the first round of the NBA playoffs because Golden State finished with the sixth best record in the conference.

In the first game of the series, Green contributed 7 points, 7 rebounds, and 4 assists during a 109-105 win on April 19, 2014. But the Clippers took Game 2 on April 21, 2014, in a decisive 138-98 win; Green did finish with 11 points, shooting 57.1 percent from the field. Green followed that up with 13 points, 11 rebounds, and 4 blocks as a reserve, but the Warriors dropped Game 3 at home by a score of 98-96 on April 24, 2014. The Warriors tied the series with a 118-97 victory on April 27, 2014, when Green scored only 4 points as a starter. He would finish the series strong despite the Clippers defeating the Warriors in seven games to advance in the playoffs.

During Golden State's Game 5 loss, 113-103, in Los Angeles on April 29, 2014, Green had 10 points and 11 rebounds. He had a much better game during the 100-99 win in Game 6 at home on May 1, 2014. Despite making just 33.3 percent of his field goal attempts, Green still had 14 points with 14 rebounds for a double-double, while also collecting 5 steals and

4 assists to help Golden State tie the series at 3-3. Green had the best postseason game of his young career during Game 7 of the first-round series on May 3, 2014, in a 126-121 loss in Los Angeles; he went 9 of 13 from the field with 5 of 8 from behind the 3-point arc to finish with 24 points, along with 7 rebounds, 3 assist, 2 steals, and 2 blocks.

While Golden State felt they could have had a deeper run in the postseason, it was still a strong season for a young team. Green finished with increased numbers after playing in all 82 games in the regular season; he averaged 6.2 points, 5 rebounds, and almost 2 assists per game; nearly doubling his statistics from his rookie season.

2014-15 Season

Shortly after the end of the previous season, the Warriors had let go of Mark Jackson and brought in former NBA champion player Steve Kerr to become the team's head coach – his first attempt after having stepped down as the general manager and president of the Phoenix Suns a few years prior and he had just sold the last little bit of his stock in the Suns' franchise. Kerr was going to develop his game plan based on some of the great coaching minds he played for during his years in Chicago with Phil Jackson – specifically the triangular offense – the pace that Gregg Popovich used in San Antonio and the tempo style made famous by Alvin Gentry in Phoenix.

But that wasn't the only change for the Warriors, as David Lee suffered another left hamstring strain during the later parts of the NBA preseason and was sidelined during about 24 of Golden State's first 25 games of the season. This allowed Green to get more starting time and he maintained that role for almost the remainder of the season. That's because Green was making big contributions early on in the season.

During the first seven games of the season, Green averaged about 13.6 points per game; that included having a double-double in the season opener on October 29, 2014, during a 95-77 win in Sacramento, where he had 12 points and 10 rebounds. He set a career-high scoring mark with 24 points after converting on 8 of 13 field goal attempts (4 of 8 from 3-point range) in addition to collecting 8 rebounds and 5 assists. He surpassed the 20-point mark again in Golden State's first loss of the season, 107-95, in Phoenix on November 9, 2014; Green converted on 50 percent from the field for 22 points in the game, with 9 rebounds and 4 blocks. The Warriors lost again the next night at home to the San Antonio Spurs, 113-100.

After the consecutive losses early in the season, the Warriors went on a 16-game winning streak, during which Green averaged a little more than 13 points per game. At the beginning of the streak, during a 107-99 win over the Brooklyn Nets on November 13, 2014, Green had 17 points, 8 rebounds, and 7 assists while making 50 percent of his field goal attempts. On November 30, 2014, Green made 62.5 percent of his 3-

point shots (5 of 8) and had 20 points in the 104-93 win in Detroit. But he was also getting large numbers in the rebounding category during this run, including 14 on December 4, 2014, against New Orleans in a 112-85 win, when Green also had 14 points after shooting 46.2 percent from the field.

Green's best game offensively came on December 6, 2014, during a 112-102 win on the road against the Chicago Bulls; he was effective from long range with 7 of 13 made shots from behind the 3-point arc and 11 of 20 overall from the field to finish the game with 31 points; Green also added 7 rebounds, 4 steals, 3 assists, and 3 blocks in one of those rare games he outscored even Stephen Curry.

His third year in the league was proving to be a season of firsts for Green. On January 2, 2015, he collected his first triple-double in the NBA during the Warriors' 126-105 home win over the Toronto Raptors – his final statistic line shows 16 points, 13 assists, and 11 rebounds and he made 50 percent of his field goal attempts. Green came close to duplicating that feat with 10 points, 11 rebounds, and 8 assists during Golden State's 112-94 win over Cleveland on January 9, 2015. Nearly a month later, Green had a career high record of 20 rebounds – 10 on offense and 10 on defense – during one of Golden State's few losses, 124-116 to Atlanta, on February 6, 2015.

While his offensive numbers were growing, Green was also standing out defensively, as shown by a season-high 6 steals collected in a 110-97 win over Minnesota on December 27, 2014. That was a little more than a week after he had a season-high 5 blocked shots on defense on December 16, 2014, during the Warriors' 105-98 loss in Memphis. Near the last half of the regular season, Green had three games where he had 5 steals each on February 26, 2015, against Cleveland (110-99 loss), on March 14, 2015, against the New York Knicks (125-94 win) and on March 16, 2015, against the Los Angeles Lakers (108-105 win).

Kerr's mix of plays and styles from Popovich, Jackson, and Gentry worked well as Golden State finished with a record of 67-15 and the Pacific Division crown. It was also good for the best record in the Western Conference and the league overall, so they were the top overall seed entering the NBA playoffs; their first-round-series was against the New Orleans Pelicans who happened to be last place in the Southwest Division (all teams finished above the.500 mark).

While the Pelicans had a winning record in a competitive Western Conference, they were still the eighth seed and they were swept in four games as Golden State advanced easily into the next round. Green averaged 15.8 points and 12.8 rebounds during the opening playoff series against New Orleans – including having 22 points, 10 rebounds, and 8 assists during the series-clinching win, 109-98, on April 25, 2015. It was a game in which Green made 64.3 percent of his field goal attempts, including 3 of 6 from 3-point range.

The Memphis Grizzlies provided a little more of a challenge for the Warriors after the Game 1 victory, 101-86, on May 3, 2015, when Green scored 16 points thanks to converting 4 of 8 from 3-point range. But Memphis took Games 2 and 3 before the Warriors won the last three to end the series in six games. During the second-round series, Green had 16 points and 10 rebounds in the Game 4 win, 101-84, on May 11, 2015. During the series-clinching win on May 15, 2015, Green was one of five players to score in double figures with 16 points and 12 rebounds (Curry led the team, again, with 32 points).

The Warriors found themselves facing the Houston Rockets in the Western Conference Finals; Golden State won the first three games of the series. While Curry's duo with Klay Thompson was a big reason for this playoff run, Green had some key games of his own, including having a near triple-double in the first game on May 19, 2015, where he had 13 points, 12 rebounds, and 8 assists in the 110-106 win. After notching 12 points, 8 rebounds, and 7 assists in the Game 2 victory on May 21, 2015, Green had a double-double with 17 points and 13 rebounds to support Curry's 40 points in the Warriors' 115-80 win on May 23, 2015. Green had 21 points, 15 rebounds and 5 blocks in Game 4 on May 25, 2015, but the Rockets avoided the sweep with a 128-115 win at home in Texas. Yet Golden State completed the inevitable with a 104-90 win two days later to clinch the series after five games and advance to the NBA Finals – Green had just 9 points with 13 rebounds in the fifth game.

The NBA Finals featured the rising young stars of the Warriors against the proclaimed "King" of the league, LeBron James, and the Cleveland Cavaliers. While Curry was once again the star of the championship series, Green had some big games of his own, starting with 12 points in the Game 1 victory, 108-100, on June

4, 2015. Cleveland took the next two games of the series, with James scoring 39 and 40 points, while Curry had just 19 and 27 in those two games. But Golden State showed they were the strong teamer after tying the series at 2-2 with a 103-82 win on June 11, 2015; Green had 17 points, 7 rebounds, and 6 assists to support 22 points each from Curry and Andre Iguodala. After scoring 16 points and 9 rebounds in the 104-91 win to give Golden State the series lead, Green had an impressive triple-double with 16 points, 11 rebounds, and 10 assists, making 46.2 percent of his field goal attempts. Along with 25 points from Curry and Iguodala, Golden State was able to defeat Cleveland 105-97 to clinch the NBA Championship on June 16, 2015.

The game was historic for a number of reasons beyond Golden State winning their first league title since 1975. Green became just one of six players in league history to have a triple-double in a game that clinched the NBA Championship. Doing so put Green among some of the NBA's biggest names like Magic Johnson, Larry Bird, Tim Duncan, and LeBron James.

At the end of the season, Green would finish with per game averages that were nearly double what he did during the season prior – 11.7 points, 8.2 rebounds, 3.7 assists, 1.6 steals, and 1.3 blocks. He was also shooting 44.3 percent from the field, with 33.7 percent of his 3-pointers converted throughout his 79 starts in the regular season. Considering that a majority of his rebounds were collected on defense, it was no surprise that Green was one of the first team members of the league's All-Defensive Team; joining a roster with San Antonio's Kawhi Leonard, Memphis' Tony Allen, and the Clippers' Chris Paul and DeAndre Jordan.

Moving Forward (2015-16 Season)

After having such a great third season in the NBA, Green's contract was expiring in the offseason. Even though he wasn't the offensive threat that Stephen Curry is, he was still able to show his overall value to the Warriors and their appreciation for his improved play was rewarded when they signed Green to a new five-year contract that was worth about $82 million. With the team Golden State had built over the past few years, they entered the current season as a favorite to repeat as NBA Champions.

As of this writing, Green has played at a level worthy of the contract he signed. During the first 10 games, Green he averaged nearly 12 points and 8 rebounds and led the team in assists with about 6.6 per game. When the Warriors set the record for the best start to an NBA season with a 16-0 mark after a 111-77 win over the Lakers, Green made 7 of 11 from the field to finish with 18 points, 7 rebounds, and 5 assists. It wasn't long after that when Green had his third career triple-double during the Warriors' 135-116 win on the road against the Phoenix Suns on November 27, 2015; he had 14 points, 10 rebounds, and 10 assists in the contest. In Golden State's next game on November 28, 2015, during a 120-101 win over Sacramento, Green had another triple-double with 13 points, 12 assists, and 11 rebounds.

Just beyond the halfway part of the 2015-16 NBA season, Green has had 18 double-doubles and nine triple-doubles. His best overall game came on January 2, 2016, during a 111-108 win at home over the Denver Nuggets, when Green scored 29 points to lead the team, making 10 of 16 from the field and 5 of 9 from behind the 3-point arc. He also had 17 total rebounds (13 on defense) and another 14 assists. With games like that, it has been no surprise to see Green receive his first NBA All-Star Game nomination during the current season, where he joined Golden State teammates Curry and Thompson.

There have been a lot of comparisons of the 2015-16 Golden State Warriors to the 1995-96 Chicago Bulls, who had the best record in NBA history with 72 wins. But that team featured legendary names like Michael Jordan and Scottie Pippen. While the modern Warriors had a better start to their season, it is hard to imagine any team in the NBA surpassing that win total while finishing with single-digit losses in a conference that features extremely tough competition with the San Antonio Spurs and the Los Angeles Clippers.

Moving forward, it will be interesting to see if Green can help the Warriors become the greatest team in terms of wins and losses. Then again, he and the rest of the Golden State squad would probably prefer just winning another NBA Championship in exchange for that win-loss record; which is looking very likely at the moment.

Chapter 4: U.S. National Team

Before he ever walked onto a court in the NBA, Green was a member of the U.S. men's national team that competed in the 2011 Summer Universidad in Shenzhen, Guangdong, China, in mid-August. The competition took place during a multi-sport event in which collegiate athletes represent their countries in competitions organized by the International University Sports Federation (FISU). The event has also been given the common English name of the World University Games and is second only to the Olympic Games in international prestige.

Green was part of an all-star college team that included Notre Dame's Tim Abromaitis, Syracuse's Scoop Jardine, and Alabama's JaMychal Green. But Draymond Green was considered a decent member coming out of Tom Izzo's Michigan State University program. He didn't disappoint in his first game of the Pool D play on August 13, 2011, during a 108-67 win over Mexico; he scored 10 points, converting on 3 of 4 field goal attempts (including 1 basket from 3-point range) while also collecting 3 rebounds, 2 steals, and 1 assist in about 16½ minutes on the court. Green spent a little more time on the court in the team's second game of the tournament (17:15 to be exact), when he made 40 percent of his field goal attempts and 4 of 6 free throws to finish with 9 points, 2 rebounds and 2 assists as a minor contributor in the United States' 102-53 win over Hungary on August 14, 2011.

In their third game of the tournament's pool play on August 15, 2011, Green had his first double-double of the Universidad competition by scoring 12 points and collecting 12 rebounds, as the United States defeated South Korea, 112-68. Green was efficient; only on the court for less than 16 minutes, he made 5 of 8 field goal attempts and also had 4 steals and 3 assists. It was a team win, as they were led by JaMychal Green's 17 points, followed by Jardine's 16 points, and 14 points from both Ashton Gibbs and Trevor Mbakwe. The United States continued their dominant play as they defeated Finland 124-64, on August 17, 2011. While Green led the team with 9 rebounds, he struggled offensively, making just 2 of 8 from the field (1 of 4 from behind the 3-point line) to finish with 6 total points.

The United States finished its pool play schedule with a perfect, undefeated 5-0 record after defeating Israel, 94-85, on August 18, 2011, in a game where Green made just 2 of 5 field goal attempts and 2 of 3 free throws to put up 6 points, 5 rebounds, 2 assists, and 1 steal. The Americans were generally expected to continue their dominance. However, they ran into a decent team from Lithuania; one that included Gediminas Orelik, who scored 19 points, and double-digit scoring from Marius Valukonis (11), Gediminas Zyle (10), and Edgaras Stanionis (10) during the first round of bracket play on August 20, 2011.

The United States lost a close game, 76-74, to Lithuania in a contest where John Jenkins led the U.S. with 17 points, followed by Ashton Gibbs with 16 points, and Trevor Mbakwe led the team with 10 rebounds. Green made 3 of 8 field goal attempts (missing all 3 from beyond the 3-point line) to finish with 6 points, 7 rebounds, and 3 steals. The loss put the Americans in the loser's bracket where they were not even be able to advance to the bronze medal round. Instead, they found themselves playing Romania on August 21, 2011, where Green had one of his best games to help the United States earn the victory, 94-73. Green played a little more than 19 minutes while making 7 of 10 field goal attempts (2 of 3 from 3-point range) and had a total of 16 points while also collecting 4 rebounds, 4 assists, and 1 steal.

The final game of the 2011 Summer Universidad was an 86-83 win over Germany on August 22, 2011. It wasn't the strong type of performance that basketball fans usually saw from the Michigan State Spartan, as he made just 1 out of his 6 total field goal attempts for only 4 points; he missed all of his attempts from behind the 3-point line. Green didn't have a completely bad game, as he recorded 6 rebounds, 3 assists, and 1 steal.

The United States finished fifth in the men's basketball tournament and Green averaged 8.6 points, 6 rebounds, 2.1 assists, and 1.6 steals in the 8 games he played; he made 46.3 percent from the field and 33.3 percent from 3-point distance. It was the only tournament in which he has worn the red, white and blue, but it might not be his last time.

In 2014, Green was named a member of the USA Basketball Select Team roster in July 2014 to be part of a training session with the men's national team during a training camp held July 28-31, 2014, at Mendenhall Center on the campus of the University of Nevada-Las Vegas in Las Vegas, Nevada. Along with Green, other notable players included Doug McDermott (Chicago Bulls), Victor Oladipo (Orlando Magic), and Tim Hardaway, Jr. (New York Knicks).

Fast forward to August 2015: Green was one of four Golden State Warriors who were invited to try out for the U.S. men's national team that will be competing at the 2016 Summer Olympics in Rio de Janeiro, Brazil. A three-day minicamp was held, similar to the one in

2014 that Green was a part of, in Las Vegas, Nevada. He was joined by teammates Stephen Curry, Harrison Barnes, and Klay Thompson.

Everything led to the 2015 USA Basketball Showcase Game held on August 13, 2015. Teams were split between USA Blue and USA White. Green was part of the latter, along with Golden State teammate Thompson and a number of other young NBA stars whom Green had become familiar with during the Western Conference Playoffs the past few years; including DeMarcus Cousins of the Sacramento Kings, Kawhi Leonard of the San Antonio Spurs and Blake Griffin of the L.A. Clippers. The white team got the victory in the showcase, 134-128, with Cousins leading the team with 24 points and Mason Plumlee (Portland Trail Blazers) scoring 20 points of his own. While Green scored just 2 points, he led the USA White squad with 10 assists and collected 4 rebounds.

Months later, Green was listed as one of the 30 finalists to be named to the men's team that will travel to Brazil for the 2016 Summer Olympics, which shows how he has evolved to join an impressive list of all-star quality players like Jimmy Butler, James Harden, Kevin Durant and LeBron James. Now the head coach, current Duke University legend Mike Krzyzewski, has a very difficult choice to make when cutting the roster down to just 12 players who will be flown down in the summer months. While it might be difficult for Green to be selected from such a talented pool of basketball talents, the fact that he made this list is a good sign of how he has developed his overall basketball performance in the past few seasons at Golden State.

Chapter 5: Personal Life

After he was drafted to play for the Golden State Warriors in 2012, Green had to move outside of that 70-mile radius in the state of Michigan that he had known from his childhood in Saginaw to his college days in East Lansing on the campus of Michigan State University. Of course, the other major change in his life was that he had a large amount of money with a new professional basketball contract. The interesting thing is that he could have easily lived in pricey condominium or high-rise apartment in the San Francisco area where other Warrior players were residing.

But Green went with a much quieter apartment in a smaller town of Emeryville, California. Sure, he could have lived in the same San Francisco neighborhood as Stephen Curry since his three-year contract was worth about $2.6 million – but he told Rusty Simmons of the *San Francisco Chronicle* that he was not the wealthiest person growing up in Saginaw and that he wasn't going to change his life style just because he was now a millionaire playing professional basketball.

That background came from growing up in a Midwestern town that was once a key industrial hub but was feeling the effects of the auto industry's decline. His parents, Mary Barbers and Wallace Davis, did the best that they could. Barbers divorced Davis and married Raymond Green when Draymond was just 12 years old. Raymond would become Draymond's stepfather while raising him and Draymond's two brothers, Torrian Harris and Braylon Green, along with three sisters, LaToya Barbers and Jordan and Gabby Davis. His brother Torrian was also a decent basketball player who played two seasons with the University of Nebraska-Omaha.

Back during Green's childhood, his mother, Barbers-Green, was almost like a police officer who made all of the kids in her home obey the rules of a nightly curfew. She caught Green cheating on a science test while he was in the ninth grade at Saginaw High School – which led to her taking away all of his privileges, taking down his bed, signing him up for summer school classes and not allowing him to go to an AAU basketball tournament; which she relented on shortly afterward.

While Green developed into a good basketball player, he was also known for more than just his skills on the court. In fact, his mother also gave him the nickname "the heckler" during his childhood since he was always trash-talking on the basketball court well before his professional days at Golden State and even before his college days at Michigan State. This was revealed as his mother started to gain some fame on social media for posting comments on her Twitter account while watching Green's games with the Warriors. His mother told Ann Killion that trash-talking was almost a way of life for Green, who did it as a way of having a small bit of fun in that little city of Saginaw.

Despite all of the hard times in Saginaw, Green was able to elevate himself to earning a scholarship to play at Michigan State and to the NBA. With all of his success in basketball, Green has used the stage to identify himself as a man who follows the Christian faith, which might explain some of his philanthropic decisions he made after signing that five-year, $82-million contract after his third year in the NBA.

Chapter 6: Giving Back to MSU

Green's passion for the Michigan State Spartans was never a secret and it was noted how it dated back to his childhood; his aunt Annette had played for the Spartans women's basketball team back in the day. He grew up wearing the green and white while watching hometown hero Jason Richardson of Saginaw help Michigan State win the 2000 National Championship under head coach Tom Izzo.

That love grew as Green was able to play for the Spartans and developed his game over the four seasons he played collegiately; which yielded three Big Ten Conference Championships and two appearances in the Final Four, and he won the conference's Player of the Year Award. But even during the time he has played professionally for the Golden State Warriors, Green never forgot his roots. After Green saw a lot more green in his bank account after signing his $82 million contract to stay with the Warriors, he spent some of that newfound wealth to give back to a program that helped him become the basketball player he is today.

In September of 2015, Green returned to the college campus in East Lansing and gave the MSU Athletics Department a check for $3.1 million to assist the men's basketball team. He spoke about what it meant to give back to Michigan State during a press conference held at the Breslin Center – his home court for those four years with the Spartans – and sat next to his former coach, the school's president, Lou Anna K. Simon, and the athletic director, Mark Hollis. He called the donation just a small gesture of thanks to Michigan State University.

It was one of the largest monetary donations any professional athlete has ever given to any college or university. The only person to do more was when professional baseball player (and former Detroit Tiger) Curtis Granderson donated $5 million to the University of Illinois-Chicago about two years prior to help the school to construct a brand-new baseball stadium. Green did provide the highest gift anyone gave to the MSU athletics program, but not by much since basketball legend Earvin Johnson – known best as Magic – donated about $3 million toward the football stadium's north end zone renovation.

Green's donation actually came at a good time for the university, since it was making a fundraising push to reach $262 million and Green helped with that. In addition to Johnson also giving money; others who have recently donated funds to the school include NBA's Steve Smith's $2.5 million to help build the Clara Bell Smith Center, which is named after the basketball star's mother.

As for what Green's donation would be used for, the school announced that they would spend about $1 million toward a new Draymond Green Strength and Conditioning Center within the Breslin Center. The rest of the money was put toward an endowment to help provide scholarship money to student-athletes who need the financial assistance.

Green timed the donation announcement just perfectly for the school's biggest recruiting weekend of the season, which featured the Spartan football team hosting the Oregon Ducks on September 12, 2015; that ended in a thrilling 31-28 win to help spark the Spartans' push for an appearance in the College Football National Championship Playoffs months later. During the win over the Ducks, Green walked the sidelines as a special guest – one of the perks of donating $3.1 million to a school's athletic program, not only because he was a member of the defending NBA Champions.

Chapter 7: Legacy in the NBA

Green never got a lot of attention coming into the league except for those who tracked his career in East Lansing. But, by the time his third season in the NBA ended with Golden State winning the league championship, fans across the world started to take notice of Green. In the weeks leading up to the NBA Finals, it was noted how well he was able to guard against the NBA's best point guards, centers, and forward in addition to collecting his high number of steals and blocks. This was all on top of how well he was playing as an offensive threat who complemented the play of Stephen Curry and Klay Thompson.

After all, having a lot of depth helps teams in any professional sport win championships. Not only did the Warriors select a player who could score and play great defense, they found someone in the second round of the 2012 NBA Draft who had the type of work ethic that helped him become a starter in East Lansing and eventually one of the reasons the Spartans had two Final Four appearances in his four seasons at Michigan State.

Considering how he is likely to have 10 or more triple-doubles by the end of the current 2015-16 NBA season, there is a good chance that Green will continue to grow even more. Some NBA experts believe that Green might currently be the best center in the league. If he maintains his averages above 16 points and more than 10 rebounds per game, there is a good chance those experts might be right. When looking at how Green evolved in college and how fast he progressed into a starting role with the Warriors, fans in the Bay Area in California have a lot of expectations for his future with the team.

Final Word/About the Author

I was born and raised in Norwalk, Connecticut. Growing up, I could often be found spending many nights watching basketball, soccer, and football matches with my father in the family living room. I love sports and everything that sports can embody. I believe that sports are one of most genuine forms of competition, heart, and determination. I write my works to learn more about influential athletes in the hopes that from my writing, you the reader can walk away inspired to put in an equal if not greater amount of hard work and perseverance to pursue your goals. If you enjoyed *Draymond Green: The Inspiring Story of One of Basketball's Best All-Around Forwards,* please leave a review! Also, you can read more of my works on *Colin Kaepernick, Aaron Rodgers, Peyton Manning, Tom Brady, Russell Wilson, Michael Jordan, LeBron James, Kyrie Irving, Klay Thompson, Stephen Curry, Kevin Durant, Russell Westbrook, Anthony Davis, Chris Paul, Blake Griffin, Kobe Bryant, Joakim*

Noah, Scottie Pippen, Carmelo Anthony, Kevin Love, Grant Hill, Tracy McGrady, Vince Carter, Patrick Ewing, Karl Malone, Tony Parker, Allen Iverson, Hakeem Olajuwon, Reggie Miller, Michael Carter-Williams, John Wall, James Harden, Tim Duncan, Steve Nash, Jimmy Butler, Marc Gasol, Dirk Nowitzki and Pau Gasol in the Kindle Store. If you love basketball, check out my website at claytongeoffreys.com to join my exclusive list where I let you know about my latest books and give you lots of goodies.

Like what you read? Please leave a review!

I write because I love sharing the stories of influential people like Draymond Green with fantastic readers like you. My readers inspire me to write more so please do not hesitate to let me know what you thought by leaving a review! If you love books on life, basketball, or productivity, check out my website at claytongeoffreys.com to join my exclusive list where I let you know about my latest books. Aside from being the first to hear about my latest releases, you can also download a free copy of *33 Life Lessons: Success Principles, Career Advice & Habits of Successful People*. See you there!

Clayton

References

1. "Draymond Green Bio." *MSUSpartans.com*. Michigan State University. N.d. Web.
2. Various Game Articles. *MSUSpartans.com*. Michigan State University. N.d. Web.
3. "Saginaw High School 07-08 Basketball Schedule." *MaxPreps.com*. MaxPreps. N.d. Web.
4. "Draymond Green." *Rivals*.com. Yahoo. N.d. Web.
5. "Draymond Green Player Profile." RealGM Basketball. N.p. n.d. Web.
6. "USA Basketball Names 13 Players to 2014 USA Men's Select Team." SLAMonline. N.p. 23 July 2014. Web.
7. "Warriors Foursome Competing at USA Basketball Minicamp." *Golden State Warriors*. NBA.com. 12 Aug. 2015. Web.
8. "Box Score: 2015 Men's National Team Showcase." *USA Basketball*. USA Basketball. 13 Aug. 2015. Web.
9. Harris, Jeff. "Very Hard Task Ahead for USA Basketball Head Coach Mike Krzyzewsk – Choosing the 12-Man Roster for the 2016 U.S. Olympic Men's Basketball Team." *Crossmap Christian News*. N.p. 22 Jan. 2016. Web.
10. "Draymond Green." *NBADraft.net*. Sports Phenoms, Inc. n.d. Web.
11. "2012 NBA Draft Board." *NBA.com: Draft 2012*. National Basketball Association, n.d. Web.
12. "Draymond Green." *Basketball-Reference.com*. Sports Reference LLC, n.d. Web.
13. Simmons, Rusty. "Warriors rookie seems down to Earth. *SFGate.com*. San Francisco Gate, 4 Oct. 2012. Web.
14. "Expressions of Faith." YouTube.com. YouTube. July 2013, Web (Video), 18 July 2013.
15. Killion, Ann. "For Draymond Green, Trash-talking is a Family Tradition." *SFGate.com*. San Francisco Gate. 23 April 2015. Web.
16. Simmons, Rusty. "For Warriors, Green's work paying off." *SFGate.com*. San Francisco Gate. 2 Dec. 2013. Web.
17. Gonzalez, Antonio. "Kerr coming to New York as an All-Star coach with Warriors." *SFGate.com*. San Francisco Gate. 10 Feb. 2015. Web.
18. Rexrode, Joe. "Draymond Green donates $3.1 million to MSU athletics." Freep.com. Detroit Free Press. 10 Sept. 2015. Web.

Made in the USA
San Bernardino, CA
10 June 2016